OKRA CULTIVATION

HOW TO GROW OKRA FROM SEED

By Lucky James

Table of Contents

Chapter one: Introduction to Okra farming

One of the most important vegetable that is grown worldwide for its green tender fruit is Okra. Okra is used as a vegetable in many ways. This particular crop is an annual crop that belong to the family Malvaceae. Okra is seen as an important vegetable in areas like India, West Africa, Brazil and the United States. Okra as a plant is really very rich in vitamins, calcium, potassium and other minerals matter. Okra as a vegetable can be fried and cooked with necessary ingredients. Okra has a lot of health benefits. The following are some of the health benefits of Okra.

1. Okra as a vegetable helps to aid digestion.
2. Okra as a vegetable is a low calorie food.
3. Okra can really helps the body detoxify itself.
4. Okra really helps to control cholesterol levels.
5. Okra can help to fight cancer in the body.
6. Okra can help to boosts the immune system.
7. Okra really help to support fertility and healthy pregnancy in women.
8. Eating Okra helps to stabilizes the blood sugar levels.
9. Okra really helps to prevent diabetes.
10. Okra also helps to prevent kidney disease.

11. Eating Okra can help to reduce asthma symptoms.

12. Eating Okra can really give you a shiny, bouncy hair.

13. Okra is really good for the brain.

14. Okra is also good for the eye health.

15. Okra helps to support strong bones.

16. Eating Okra is really good for the skin.

17. Okra is really a great source of vegetable protein for the body.

18. Okra really support ulcer healing.

There are a lot health benefits of Okra. Starting an Okra farm can be very profitable if it is done in a proper way. There is high demand on Okra both in the international and local market. On this book we are going to discuss everything about Okra cultivation. We are going to look at the step by step on how to grow Okra from seed.

Chapter two: Different varieties of Okra

There are different varieties of Okra. The following are some of the different varieties of Okra.

1. The Red Burgundy Okra variety: This particular variety is a four feet plant that have green leaves and burgundy stems. This variety matures between 52 to 60 days. Below is the image of the variety.

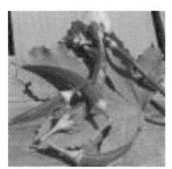

2. The Clemson Spineless 80 Okra variety: The Clemson Spineless 80 Okra variety is the most popular variety in the market. This variety is 3 to 5 foot tall. They can mature between 48 to 60 days. Below is the image of the variety.

3. The Emerald Okra variety: This particular variety is also known as Emerald Green Velvet. The Emerald Okra variety is about 5 to 8 foot tall with green-gray lightly lobed leaves. This variety can mature between 55-65 days. Below is the image of the variety.

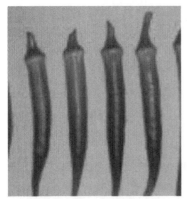

4. The Lee Okra variety: The Lee Okra variety produces dwarf plants that are between 2.5 to 3 feet tall. This particular variety can mature between 45 to 55 days. Below is the image of the variety.

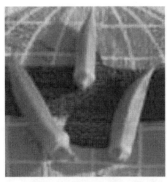

5. The Long Pod Green Okra variety: The Long Pod Green Okra variety is a 4 to 6 foot sturdy plant that produce long slender lightly ribbed attractive dark-green spineless pods. The Long Pod Green Okra variety can mature between 52 to 65 day. Below is the image of the variety.

Chapter three: How to grow Okra from seed

The land preparation for the Okra plant

The first stage is the preparation of the land. Try and make sure the land is tilled properly. Make sure you remove all the rock and stone. Also make sure that they land is exposed to adequate sunshine, whether is a small garden or a large piece of land just make sure that there are no shades that prevent sufficient exposure of the soil surface to sunlight. One thing about Okra plant is that they does poorly on a waterlogged soil so it is very important that the soil being used is well drained. Don't forget to evaluate the soil in terms of fertility before adding manure.

The Soaking of the Okra Seeds

One thing about Okra is that they are easy to grow but the seeds really have a hard coat that can really slow the germination. One of the ways to speed up the process is by soaking the seeds overnight in warm water before planting them. Also if you wrap the Okra seeds in a moist paper towel it also work well.

The Okra seed rate

In the area of the seed rate about 20 kg seed/ha is required for summer season crop, why about 10 kg seed/ha is needed for rainy season crop.

The sowing and spacing method

Try and make sure that the Okra seed are sown on ridges with a distance of 60 cm between rows and 15-30 cm between plants.

The Irrigation of the Okra plant

To actually facilitate a better germination there must be enough moisture in the soil. Try as much as possible to make sure that the Okra plants are irrigated at an interval of 5-6 days in summer and whenever required in rainy season.

Applying manure and Fertilizer to the Okra

Try as much as possible to make sure that the farmland is incorporated with a well rotten farm yard manure @ 25 t/ha one month before bed preparation. Make sure that 25 kg of nitrogen per hectare is thoroughly mixed in the soil before sowing 25 kg each of phosphorus and potash. Also try to ensure that another dose of 25 kg of nitrogen per hectare is given at the time of flowering and fruit setting.

Chapter four: Pest and disease control in Okra

Okra plant is like any other plant that also face some pest and disease challenges. The following are some of the pest and disease that attack Okra plant.

1. The charcoal rot disease of okra:

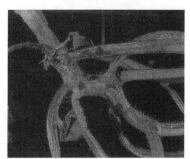

The Symptoms: What you will see is the discoloration of stem at the soil line. Another thing again is that the cankers on the stem may spread upwards. The Okra leaves may begin to wilt and drop from the plant.

The cause: Fungus

How to manage and control it: You need to rotate the crop to a non-host in other to reduce the build-up of inoculum in the soil. Try as much as possible to avoid water stress to plants by irrigating when it is required.

2. The fusarium wilt disease of okra:

The Symptoms: What you will observe is the wilting of cotyledons and seedling leaves. You will observe that the cotyledons has become chlorotic at the edges and then necrotic. You will also observe that the older plants has exhibit a symptoms of wilting and leaf chlorosis. By peraventure if the infection is very severe the Okra plants will become stunted and may be killed. You will also observe that the vascular system of the infected Okra plants has become discolored and can only be seen by cutting the stem.

The cause: Fungus

How to manage and control it: Try as much as possible to use certified, disease-free seed. Try to also plant varieties that has higher resistance to the disease in areas that has a history of Fusarium diseases. You can also fumigate the soil, this may help to reduce the incidence of the disease.

3. The Powdery mildew disease on Okra:

The symptoms: What you will observe is a powdery white covering on the leaves. In some case the patches may coalesce to cover the entire Okra plant. By peraventure if the Okra plant is heavily infected the leaves may roll upward and appear scorched.

The cause: Fungus

How to manage and control it: Try as much as possible to use overhead irrigation (this will wash the fungus from the leaves and it will reduce viability). Make sure you plant the crop as early as possible. You can also apply the appropriate fungicides to control the disease.

4. The Southern blight disease of okra:

The symptoms: What you will observe is a sudden wilting of leaves. There will be yellowing foliage. You will also be seeing a browning stem above and below the soil. You will be seeing browning branches. In some case the stem may be covered with fan-like mycelial mat.
The cause: Fungus

How to manage and control it: Try and remove all infected Okra plants. Make sure you avoid overcrowding of the Okra plants to promote air circulation. Make sure you rotate the crops with a less susceptible plants. Make sure you also plow crop debris deep into the soil.

5. The White mold disease on Okra:

The symptoms: What you will observe is that the flowers will be covered in white cottony fungal growth. What you will see is a small, circular, dark green, water-soaked lesions on the pods leaves and branches which will enlarge and become slimy.
The cause: Fungus

How to manage and control it: Make sure you rotate the crops with a non-hosts like cereals and corn. Try as much as possible to plant the rows parallel to the direction of the prevailing winds in other to prevent the spread of disease from secondary hosts nearby. Make sure you avoid excessive nitrogen fertilizer. Also make sure you use a wide row spacing.

6. The Enation leaf curl disease on Okra:

The symptoms: What you will observe on the lower surface of the leaves is a small pin head enations. There will be a reduction in leaf size. You will see the leaves appearing thicker and leathery. There will be production of few deformed fruits.

The cause: Virus

How to manage and control it: Try as much as possible to remove all the infected Okra plant and burn them to avoid further spread of disease. You can also use a yellow sticky trap to monitor the whiteflies population. In a situation where the whiteflies infestation is more you can spray a suitable insecticide.

7. The yellow vein mosaic disease on Okra:

The Symptoms: One the symptoms of this disease is that the infected leaves will show an alternate patches of green and yellow. You will observe that the veins are becoming clear and chlorotic. There will be a time when the stems and the leaf stalk will be distorted. What you will observe again is that the fruits will become yellowish green in color and small in size.

The cause: Virus

How to manage and control it: Make sure you use resistant cultivars. Try as much as possible to sow disease free certified seeds. Try to adopt crop rotation. Make sure you keep the field free from weeds. You can also control vector with suitable insecticides.

8. The Spider mites on Okra:

The symptoms: You will see the leaves stippled with yellow. Also the leaves will appear bronzed. You will see Webb covering the leaves. You will start seeing the leaves turning yellow and begin to drop from the plant.

The Cause: Arachnid

How to manage and control it:

Try and spray the Okra plants with a strong jet of water, this can really help to reduce the buildup of spider mite populations. By peradventure if the mites really become a problem you can apply insecticidal soap to the Okra plants.

9. The Root-knot nematode on okra:

The symptoms: There will be a reduction in plant vigor. The plant will become yellow and begin to wilt in hot weather.

The Cause: Nematode

How to manage and control it: Try as much as possible to plant resistant varieties if the nematodes are known to be present in the soil. Make sure you check the roots of the plants in mid-season or sooner if the symptoms really indicate nematodes.

Chapter five: Harvesting of Okra

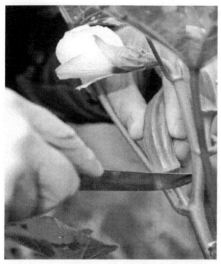

Harvesting of the Okra is the last stage. One of the good thing about Okra farming is that the pods are usually ready for harvest two months after planting. The Okra pods can be harvest four to six days after flowering and also the pods can harvested every two to three days when they have reached about 7.6–15.2 cm (3–5 in) in length. You can remove the Pods from the plant by cutting it with a sharp knife or also by snapping it from the plant.

OKRA CULTIVATION

HOW TO GROW OKRA FROM SEED

By Lucky James

Made in United States
Troutdale, OR
10/04/2023